A CHRISTMAS MIRACLE FOR

Grace

Dr. Bebe V. Villarreal
Illustrated by Elenei Rae Pulido

Print information available on the last page

Rev. date: 12/07/2018

To order additional copies of this book, contact:
Xlibris
1-888-795-4274
www.Xlibris.com
Orders@Xlibris.com

A CHRISTMAS MIRACLE FOR Grace

For all who rejoice in the story of the birth of Jesus, Our Newborn King and Savior, whose gift of love is the greatest gift of all.

It was Christmas Eve, and Grace's parents were getting ready to read the wondrous story about the birth of Jesus to Grace and her younger sister Sarah. This was Grace's favorite Christmas story.

It was snowing gently outside. The fireplace made everything quite cozy inside. Grace was a very pretty, intelligent girl who was born blind. She was unable to see the world around her. She used her remarkable imagination to help her to paint pictures in her mind.

Everyone gathered around the warm fireplace. Soon, Mother opened the Christmas book and began to read, "Mary, who was expecting a baby and Joseph, traveled a long way by donkey to Bethlehem in Judea. It was a cold night, and Mary was exhausted from the journey.

"When they reached Bethlehem, there was no place in the inn for Jesus to be born. Joseph looked everywhere. Finally, they made their way to a stable where animals were kept. There, Mary gave birth to her newborn child, and placed Him in a manger.

Father continued with the story, "Magi from the East brought gifts of gold, frankincense, and myrrh to the Newborn King. They knelt before Jesus in homage.

There were shepherds in the fields who heard a multitude of heavenly angels singing in glory to the baby Jesus. "Peace on Earth and Goodwill to all men."

As her parents read, Grace imagined that she was really present in the manger right beside little Jesus. She could smell the hay, and hear the stable animals breathing. Great wonder and delight filled her heart with warmth and love.

Grace hummed softly as she listened to the beautiful story. God had given Grace an extraordinary gift of singing. When she sang, people stopped to listen in amazement! After the wonderful Christmas story had ended, everyone went to bed.

That night, Grace had a fascinating dream. She dreamed that she was taken to Bethlehem on the mighty wings of large, beautiful angels, and her hair flew in the cold wind. She was taken to the manger where the baby Jesus was sleeping.

When they arrived, she heard the soft cooing of the Newborn King who was lying in the manger, but she could not see Him. Grace realized that stable animals were keeping the baby Jesus warm with their breath.

Suddenly, a sweet, soft voice of a lady asked, "What is your name?" "My name is Grace, she replied." "My name is Mary, and my baby's name is Jesus. Joseph is standing here beside me", she said. Grace trembled. It was Mary, the Mother of Jesus, who was speaking to her!

"Come Grace, and see my baby," Mary said. Mary held Grace's hand gently, and led her to her Infant Son. "Grace, do you wish to touch my baby?" asked Mary. "I would love to with all of my heart," Grace replied eagerly.

The instant that Grace touched the baby Jesus' face, his tiny hands, and his precious little feet, her eyesight was miraculously restored! She could see the precious Infant clearly! Tears of joy rolled down her cheeks.

"I love you with all of my heart, my little Jesus, Grace whispered to precious Jesus tearfully. I was blind, but now I can see, she said to Him. My Christmas Miracle has been done for me! Now, I would love to sing a birthday song for you".

As Grace began to sing "Silent Night," all of the radiant lights of heaven shone down brightly upon the holy manger, and upon the Infant Jesus. This was the most extraordinary Christmas that Grace had ever experienced! Her heart was bursting with joy!

She sang magnificently with all of the love that her heart contained. Mary and Joseph, the Magi, and the shepherds listened with complete humility. Peace surrounded the quiet, calm manger.

Suddenly, Grace heard the gentle flapping of wings, and she awoke from her dream! She could see everything around her!

She hurried downstairs. "Mother, Father, I can see you, and I can see you, Sarah!" Grace exclaimed with incredible happiness! Her family was thrilled and amazed with this divine miracle.

Grace was overwhelmed as she told her family about her blissful dream. "It was through the miracle that Jesus has done for me, that I can now see," she cried. I sang "Silent Night" to Our Newborn Savior, as my gift to Him," gasped Grace through her tears.

Grace and her family hugged and wept together. Grace suggested, "May we all sing "Silent Night" outside by our manger?" She and her family sang, and Grace's eyes twinkled with the greatest wonder and happiness. The entire world celebrated the infinite love of Jesus' birth that Christmas night!

Silent Night

Silent night, Holy night,
All is calm, All is bright
Round yon virgin mother and child.
Holy infant so tender and mild,
Sleep in heavenly peace.
Sleep in heavenly peace.

Silent night, Holy night,
Shepherds quake at the sight,
Glories stream from heaven afar,
Heavenly hosts sing alleluia;
Christ the Savior, is born!
Christ the Savior, is born!
Silent night, Holy night,
Son of God, Love's pure light
Radiant beams from thy holy face,
With the dawn of redeeming grace,
Jesus, Lord, at thy birth.
Jesus, Lord, at thy birth.

Lightning Source UK Ltd.
Milton Keynes UK
UKRC011352231218
334414UK00003B/28